T0124375

Dedicated to my first grandchild's parents,
Signe & Douglas Lansky.

Copyright© 2001 by Vicki Lansky
Cover Closing Design—Patent Pending

ISBN 0-916773-63-9 • UPC 607966-63901

No part of this book may be reproduced without
permission of the publisher.

Design, Production & Printing by
Pettit Network, Afton MN

Book Peddlers
15245 Minnetonka Blvd, Minnetonka, MN 55345
phone 952-912-0036 • fax 952-912-0105
www.bookpeddlers.com
book trade distributor: PGW

To order more copies
or for a copy of our catalog
call 1-800-255-3379

Printed in
Hong Kong

03 04 05 06 07 08 09 10 9 8 7 6 5 4

Save that hotel DO NOT DISTURB sign
or make your own. Use it on any door
necessary to give you and/or your baby
some of that extra needed rest.
(The trick is to sleep when
your baby does.)

Make your own baby thank-you cards. Imprint your child's foot on blank note cards. An ink pad, your sleeping child's foot and your handwritten note make a very special 'thank you.' Or use a fabric pen and write your baby's name on his or her solid color stretch outfit. Take a photo and send·out copies as your form of appreciation.

As wonderful as it is to rock your baby to sleep, it is a better idea to put your baby down when drowsy but awake. It's okay if your little one fusses for a few minutes. This gives your baby the opportunity to learn how to drift off to sleep without you. At bedtime, or during the night, your baby won't 'demand' to be rocked to sleep, unless, of course, the reason for waking is to be fed or changed.

A newborn can be bedded down on his or her back or side for the first month or two in a large, safely padded laundry basket. Use towels or a piece of supportive foam inside a pillowcase for the bottom of the basket. This is also a good impromptu infant bed when going visiting. (Never use a basket for car travel with a sleeping child.)

Babies can also be burped by being placed tummy-down across your lap. Gently pat or rub their back in an upward motion. Or place them in a sitting position on your lap while gently patting on their back.

Babies can be bathed in a face-down 'frog' position (your hand and arm supporting the chest) as well as a face up position. Experiment to find out which works best for you. If bathing your baby is a slippery proposition, consider lining the bath container with a towel. Or use cotton gloves on your hands for a better grip.

Mild cradle cap, or crust on the scalp, can be treated by light scrubbing of the area with a soft toothbrush. Add a drop or two of oil (baby or cooking) to loosen the scale. Shampoo as usual to remove flakes. Daily shampooing can have a drying effect and aggravate cradle cap.
(A baby's soft spot on top of the head can't be damaged by gentle combing or brushing.)

An aquarium in a little one's room often provides enough light in a bedroom so you don't need to turn on a light when checking or feeding your child. The movements of the fish are soothing as well as interesting to a baby.

Flannel rubber sheets are good protection on top of baby's crib sheet. They catch spit-up and drool, or as a lap pad, they protect against leaky diapers. Buy a large sheet and cut it into smaller pieces to fit your needs.

A pretty calendar with large day spaces
hung in your baby's room is a wonderful item.
Use it to record events, accomplishments or
new spoken words. It will become a
treasured diary.

If you buy gender-free colors (yellow, purple, green, etc.) in clothes and bedding for your little one, it will be easier to reuse them for subsequent babies of yours, or new cousins to come.

Stimulate a baby's mind by providing
interesting things to look at, such as:
- colorful ribbon strips tied to the grate
  of an out-of-reach, oscillating fan
- photo faces of smiling babies
- a non-breakable mirror placed
  in a crib or playpen.

A three-tiered mesh hanging basket can be handy in baby's room for storing changing supplies or clothing. It keeps things out of reach of baby, pets or siblings.

Cleaning a messy bottom is easier to do if you keep a small spray bottle of water with a drop or two of baby oil in it. Spray, then wipe the area, with a clean cloth or toilet paper. (It's also a good idea to remove baby's socks before changing a messy diaper— it will save on laundry.)

A mobile or a colorful kite hung from the
ceiling above a changing table is a good
distraction to help minimize a little one's
fidgeting during diaper changes.

Since exposure to air is the best cure for diaper rash, consider letting your baby be bare-bottomed occasionally. Use an appropriately-placed open diaper for protection underneath. Or think about using a hair dryer for a few seconds to dry baby's bottom between diaper changes. (Be sure not to use 'hot' air and be no closer than 12 inches.)

Stained baby clothes can often be revived if
you soak the item(s) in hot water to which a
half-cup of vinegar and laundry soap have
been added. Later wash as usual. Prevent
new stains and dribbles from setting by
sprinkling baking soda on those areas before
tossing clothing in the laundry hamper or
washing machine.

Store baby's outgrown clothes in empty diaper boxes or bags that match the sizes of the clothes you're packing away. It will save on re-sorting work later.

If you need some help putting baby to sleep, try white sound. This can be the sound of your vacuum, your washer or dryer, or even your kitchen faucet running. You can record such sounds on a long-running tape to play back as needed.

A good time to trim infants' nails is while they are nursing or taking a bottle, or when they are sleeping. If you put a bit of baby powder in your hand and scrape your child's nails over the powder, you'll see where you can safely cut.

Keep a special doll or toy in your baby's
crib—and only in the crib. It may be just the
thing to encourage a little one into bed at
night by knowing that special toy is there.
It can become part of the sleep ritual
you want to create.

Just because a well-fed baby, who is older
than six months, wakes at night or too early in
the morning, doesn't mean he or she is
hungry. Don't rush in. Sometimes a little one
will fuss a bit then go back to sleep.
(And sometimes, not.)

There is nothing wrong with giving a baby cold
formula, bottled breast milk or juice straight from
the refrigerator. Your little one's hands might have
a bigger problem from the coldness. Use a
'widowed' tube sock top slipped over the bottle
to keep the chill away. The sock absorbs
condensation at the same time.

Make your own baby food (after six months or so when your baby starts to eat solid food) by freezing batches of cooked, pureed fruit or unseasoned vegetables in a molded ice cube tray. (Cooked chicken or meats usually need a little broth when pureeing.) Once frozen, transfer to a freezer storage bag. Reheat (or just defrost) frozen food cubes as needed.

Hose down a food-encrusted highchair (unless it's made of wood) outside when weather permits. Or accomplish the same task by putting the highchair in your shower.

When you begin bathing your baby in the tub, protect your knees from the hard floor by using a gardener's knee pad. Remember to protect your child from bumps or a burn from the tub faucet by padding that too.

Before your baby can actively crawl, get down on all fours and crawl through the living spaces that your baby will be in. See the world from your baby's point of view in order to remove or cover up hazards from: electric outlets (which appeal to fingers); wires (that babies like to chew on); and sharp corners (which they will inevitably hit their heads on). You will be amazed at what you will see.

When your baby begins to crawl, encourage forward motion with colorful, safe, plastic objects in his or her sight line. A line of pillows on the floor is a good obstacle for a crawler to maneuver over. A small plastic beach ball is also fun for a baby to 'chase.'

Keep reading copies of one or two parenting books in your bathroom. It may be the only place to sit down and have a minute to yourself. Many a tired parent has carved out that hard-to-find private time by waking an hour before the rest of the family.

Teach mobile babies to crawl down stairs
backwards, on their tummies, or 'toesy's first,'
until they are secure enough walkers to
manage the stairs upright.

When your baby graduates to a highchair, he or she often slides down the seat. Use a sink mat (or half a bath mat, or bath skid decals) to give your baby the needed traction to stop this from accidentally happening.

(On purpose, of course, is a different matter.)

Teething babies can soothe sore gums by chewing on: frozen teething rings, chilled pacifiers, a cold damp washcloth, or a new rubber toy from a pet store. Cold or solid foods (such as a frozen bagel, a whole carrot, a frozen banana, a pineapple core or even a dog biscuit) work too, but baby needs to be monitored so a piece doesn't break off and become a choking hazard.

After a messy meal in a high chair, hold a
small bowl, half-filled (or less) with warm
water for your child's hands to play in for a
minute. Then wipe your child's face clean with
a soft baby washcloth. (Actually applying a
bit of baby oil or petroleum jelly to baby's
cheeks BEFORE eating is better yet.) This will
make clean-up fun for your little one and
easier for you.

Graduating to a cup offers you more flexibility when traveling with your little one. Yes, there are wonderful training cups available, but you can still help your child learn to drink from mini paper cups, from the side of a baby bottle with the nipple top removed or a sports bottle. Let your child practice sipping skills in the bathtub with a favorite juice. No spills to clean up!

When it's necessary to put socks and shoes
on an unwilling baby, place him or her in a
highchair with a distraction. A few Cheerios
on the tray will let you quickly and effortlessly
dress those little feet.

Do you know the poison control emergency phone number in your area? If not, call information now and program it into your phone, or write it down next to the phone(s).

Is your little one getting VERY attached to his or her baby blanket? Find a similar one and get in the habit of rotating them every week so you will: 1) have a backup, 2) allow for a longer life of a security blanket, and 3) have the option of having a CLEAN one available when your child won't part with that one-and-only.

Keep several disposable flash cameras
around the house—maybe even one in the
car—to catch those moments you might
otherwise miss. Don't forget to capture the
multi-colored mess of self-feeding.

If you have a choice when planning trips, it's a good idea to choose destinations in your same time zone. Little ones' sleeping and feeding schedules do not quickly adjust to time zone changes which means you won't be able to either.

Keep a roll or box of gallon-size plastic
storage bags in the glove compartment of your
car or, if there is room, in your baby bag.
These will come in handy for dirty diapers,
soiled clothes, or uneaten food—
just to name a few.

Hiking around with your baby in a back carrier? If it's not well padded enough for you, use some foam pipe insulation around the hard frame where needed. (That same foam is good for baby proofing sharp corners in your house.)

You can turn a backpack into your baby bag and handbag combined. This will leave your hands free to tend to your child. At the very least, consider using a fanny pack for personal items instead of a shoulder bag.

When traveling by plane, let your baby nurse, or suck on a bottle or pacifier during take-off and landing to reduce pressure on the ears by keeping the jaw working and the saliva flowing. Little ones are more susceptible to pressurization discomfort as the Eustachian tubes in their ears are narrower.

Before boarding a plane think about double-diapering or using a nighttime disposable on your child as planes are not easy places to change a diaper. (Even a sanitary napkin in a diaper can offer extra absorbency.)

To entertain and stimulate your new baby, read
Vicki Lansky's, GAMES BABIES PLAY
For the First Twelve Months.
This collection of over 100 games, songs and
activities keeps pace with your baby's growth.
For a copy of the book or a free catalog of all
her titles, call 1-800-255-3379 or visit
www.practicalparenting.com.

Duckie = Bathtime Tips

Shoes = Dressing Tips

Crib = Sleep Tips

CODE TO
NEW BABY

TIPS

Bottle = Feeding Tip

Lamb = Clean-up Tips

Moon = Other Tips

Rocker = Activity Tips